THE FOUND
Woman

"The Found Woman is not just a story- it's a mirror.
A sacred invitation to rise from the ashes of abandonment,
burnout, and buried dreams, and reclaim the woman you
were always meant to be. Through poetic prose, sacred
truths, and soul-deep storytelling, Latosha Bobo walks us
through cycles of grief, grace and glorius becoming."

LATOSHA BOBO, MBA

ISBN: 978-1-969463-93-8

Introduction

To the Woman Who's Ready to Come Home to Herself

This book is not just about my story—it's about *ours*.

It's about the girl who gave too much too soon, the wife who forgot her name, the mother who loved but felt unseen, and the woman who finally said: *enough*.

Inside these pages, you'll find truth and tenderness. Pain and power. Each chapter was written from a place of raw honesty and spiritual clarity—not to impress you, but to invite you deeper into your own becoming.

Here, you'll meet your reflections. Your questions. Your inner knowing.

You won't find a perfect woman in these pages, but you *will* find a free one. One who cried, crawled, rose, and returned to herself—*and then wrote it all down* so you wouldn't feel alone on your journey.

If you've been asking for a sign, this is it.
Welcome home.
Let's begin.

— Latosha Bobo

Prologue

Before I was found, I was constantly becoming someone else.

Becoming who they needed. Becoming who I thought I had to be to survive. To be loved. To be seen. But somewhere between the roles I played and the wounds I carried, I lost touch with the truth of who I was.

This is not a story of perfection. It's a story of peeling back the layers—the expectations, the pain, the silence—to return to a woman I didn't know I had forgotten. To become someone I didn't yet know I could be.

This is a remembrance. A rising. A reclamation.

And if you're holding these pages, I believe something inside you is ready to be found too.

Table of Contents

CHAPTER 1

The Girl I Used to Be

"Sometimes the hardest person to forgive is the version of yourself that didn't know better."

From the outside, I looked like I had it all together—straight-A student, respectful, gifted, the kind of girl teachers loved to have in class. I was quiet, didn't cause trouble, and volunteered to read out loud. At church, I led the youth with confidence, my voice strong and sure. People saw me and smiled. They saw what I was trained to show.

But inside, I was a young girl wrapped in layers of shame, silence, and confusion—searching desperately to feel seen. I lived in a two-parent household, active in church, surrounded by structure that seemed perfect to outsiders. Yet the emotional atmosphere was flat, even cold. There wasn't tension, necessarily. Just a constant undercurrent of *invisible weight*.

In our home, vulnerability was not the language we spoke. My mother was strong and busy—always working or studying, doing what had to be done. I don't remember warm hugs or late-night talks. I remember her focus. Her doing. She taught us that silence was power— *"Never let your right hand know what your left hand is doing."* Emotions weren't punished, but they were never nurtured either. I don't recall anyone telling me to stop crying—but somewhere along the way, I learned to shut it off anyway.

I remember being in kindergarten with a UTI and just going straight to bed every day until my mom finally noticed and rushed me to the hospital. I had to be admitted. I never said a word about the pain. That's how I survived—by shrinking.

At home, I kept my voice low unless I was joking. I was mouthy sometimes, but mostly, I went along with everything. I didn't ask for much. I rarely challenged anything. And when I did, I was "talking back."

I shared a bedroom with my sister, and it felt safe—but not sacred. Just another space I occupied quietly. Most days, the house was quiet too. Occasionally gospel music would play, especially on Sunday mornings, but mostly it was stillness. I learned early on how to disappear in plain sight.

In my family, I was teased for my dark skin and my hair. "Black." "Nappy head." Words that sliced deeper than they knew. I'd laugh it off or go quiet. I never cried where anyone could see. But something in me began to shrink—avoiding mirrors, hiding in baggy clothes, trying to flatten parts of me I didn't yet understand. I thought beauty meant being light-skinned and curvy. I was neither. I felt undesirable, unlovable, unseen.

That craving for visibility led me to boys—long before I understood what "being with someone" really meant. I wasn't looking for love. I was looking for acknowledgment. For attention. For any gaze that whispered, *I see you.*

At church, I led the youth. I felt chosen there. Important. Smart. That platform gave me identity—one I clung to tightly. But when I got pregnant at 15, everything changed.

It started with a missed period I tried to hide from my mom. I didn't want my business passed around the family. But she noticed and took me to my pediatrician. During the pelvic exam, I saw something shift in the doctor's face. She didn't say much, just referred us to a lab. I didn't understand what was happening.

Later, when my mom called the house, she said, "They think you might be pregnant." I brushed it off. But the following Sunday, on the way to church, she asked me plainly, "Could you be pregnant?" I was too tired to lie. "Yes," I said softly. That was it. No tears. Just silence.

She didn't scream. She didn't cry. She said, "You know your life will be different now." But something in her shifted. Within days, it felt like disappointment took over. She started to distance herself emotionally—verbally reprimanding me, like I had failed not just myself, but her too.

Before I could process what was happening, she had told the church. Not us. Not me. *Her*. The next Sunday, in the basement of our pastor's home—where services were held—the First Lady told me I could no longer teach the youth. She didn't yell. Her face was expressionless. I felt... nothing. I stood in the basement, in between Sunday school and service, and watched my identity be stripped away in silence. I was no longer the leader. I was the cautionary tale.

The shame sat heavy.

Later, when my younger sister went through something similar and I watched her be publicly cornered in the pastor's office, I understood that what I'd experienced wasn't discipline—it was spiritual humiliation. That church, which once made me feel chosen, became the birthplace of some of my deepest church hurt.

The abortion itself was hollow.

My older sister took me. We didn't speak on the way there or back. I didn't know what to expect. No one explained anything. I had never even heard the word "abortion" before. I was just told this was what had to be done.

When the procedure began, I remember hearing the sound of a vacuum, and feeling like it sucked the life out of me. My soul.

Afterward, I didn't feel sad. I didn't feel angry. I didn't feel *anything*. Just regret. For years.

I went home and acted normal. I avoided mirrors. I moved on like it hadn't happened, but inside… something had gone missing.

Only one adult made space for me in that season—my friend's mom. After the procedure, she sat next to me. She didn't judge. Didn't scold. She just said gently, *"You'll always wonder what if."* And she was right.

Back then, I believed I had messed up. That no one would ever understand. That I had to handle it alone. Looking back now, I see a 15-year-old girl who was surviving the only way she knew how. She wasn't broken. She wasn't bad. She was *searching*—for affection, for identity, for a safe place to land.

Today, I feel her in my heart. I'm sad for her—for the way she silenced herself, for the shame she carried that never belonged to her. But I'm proud of her too. She endured. She survived silent battles no one knew she was fighting.

Now, I know that I am beautiful—flaws and all. That mistakes do not define me. That the girl I used to be was never unworthy.

She just didn't know her worth yet.

The Found Woman Reflection

Affirmation: *"I forgive the girl I used to be. I honor her journey, her strength, and her desire to be loved."*

Journal Prompt: What did your younger self need to hear but never did? Write it down. Speak it out loud.

Action Step: Write a letter to your younger self. Acknowledge her pain. Thank her for surviving. Assure her that she is safe now.

Devotional: Seen by Grace

You were never invisible to God—even when the world tried to erase you, and even when you didn't know how to see yourself. You were always held. Always loved. Even when you didn't feel seen, heaven watched over you. Even when your voice was silenced, your tears were sacred. You don't have to be perfect to be worthy. You just have to be *you*.

Take a moment today to rest in that truth: *You have always mattered. Even when no one said it out loud.*

CHAPTER 2

The Illusion of Love

"When you're starving for love,
even crumbs can feel like a feast."

I didn't realize at the time that I was slowly molding myself into a version of a woman I didn't yet recognize. I wasn't quite the girl I used to be, but I wasn't the woman I was meant to become either. I was in the in-between.

He was four years older, and while that difference seemed small on paper, in reality, it felt like a wide gap. But he saw me—or at least that's how it felt. I was a young girl still figuring herself out, and being noticed by someone older made me feel important, chosen. I never asked what he saw in me because I was too busy enjoying the feeling of being seen at all.

He was into things I had been sheltered from—smoking, drinking, a certain hardness from life. His edge intrigued me. Part of me thought love had to be earned through sacrifice or survival. Maybe I thought I could save him. Maybe I thought saving him would save me.

There was no proposal during high school—just a slow blending of lives. When I gave birth to our son, we became a unit. The very same day I was discharged from the hospital, I moved in with him. From that moment on, we were doing life together.

Those early years were stable—no major highs, no dramatic lows. We traveled, we laughed, we coexisted in a version of peace. Motherhood gave me an identity I hadn't known I needed. Holding my son for the first time felt like time stopped. He was mine. My reason. My anchor. Every move I made from that point forward was with him in mind.

And yet, even in that quiet season of stability, something in me was fading. I didn't feel seen, desired, or attractive. I wasn't nurturing myself—I was surviving. Older women, some barely more than strangers, began pouring into me with wisdom I wouldn't fully understand until later. They became small glimmers of light, breadcrumbs leading me back to myself.

The Tension in the Middle

There wasn't daily conflict between him and my mother, but I always felt pulled between the two. I thought I had to choose. And I did—my mother. I wanted her at my graduation. That choice meant moving back home after leaving at 17.

The day I moved back in, my car was totaled in an accident. I took it as a sign. Still, we kept dating. I believe I conceived again on prom night. He didn't go—said he felt too old—but I spent post-prom with him. That pregnancy wasn't an accident. I thought it would redeem the shame I carried from the first abortion. I thought creating a family on purpose would fill the void.

And for a while, I did build the vision I had in mind. I was one of the few women I knew who was married to her child's father. That counted for something back then. I wore it like a badge of honor, even though it was quietly wearing me down.

A Hollow Proposal

It wasn't until Christmas Eve, two years after our son was born, that he proposed. Well… not really. I was leaving my sister's apartment, walking down the complex's walkway to ours, when I saw our toddler walking toward me, tiny hands extended, holding a ring. No words. No question. Just a gesture wrapped in surprise.

We hadn't talked about marriage. There'd been no lead-up. Just me, standing in the cold, watching a child deliver a promise his father hadn't even spoken aloud.

And yet, I said yes. Out of habit. Out of the belief that this was the next "right" thing. That a ring would solidify the family I was still desperately trying to build.

Looking back now, I know that wasn't love—it was familiarity, guilt, and the fear of facing life alone.

The Ectopic Wake-Up Call

By May 2007, I had lost both my mom's mother and my dad's mother—the most painful grief I had known. I wished I had been more present with them. Their absence shook something loose in me. I knew deep down that they wouldn't have approved of him. But I wasn't ready to walk away just yet.

That summer, a power outage swept through most of St. Louis. His apartment still had electricity. That's how I ended up back—with him, physically, emotionally, and eventually... pregnant again.

But this pregnancy was different. My body knew something was wrong. The pain in my back was unbearable. An emergency room doctor—white and dismissive—told me I was fine and sent me home with instructions to rest. But before I left, a black doctor stepped in. He started fresh and ordered a transvaginal ultrasound.

That man saved my life.

I was having an ectopic pregnancy. Surgery was scheduled for the next morning. When I woke up from the surgery, 40% of my fallopian tube was gone. He hadn't come. But my mother and my aunt were there. They showed up with gifts, love, and quiet strength. That was the day I remembered who was really in my corner.

Looking Deeper

By then, I had lost so much—my grandmothers, my sense of self, parts of my body—and yet I was still settling. Still saying yes when I wanted to scream no. Still accepting the bare minimum from a man who was supposed to love and protect both me and our son.

I had silenced my doubts, my voice, and my worth in order to keep the illusion of family alive.

As a young mother, I didn't fully become a woman until much later in life. So many parts of me were placed on pause—my dreams, my joy, my softness. I thought love required proving myself, staying silent, and sacrificing who I was for who I thought I should be.

The emotional currency he used to pull me back in was always the same: guilt, obligation, and false hope. And for a long time, I kept paying.

But now? Now I see that love doesn't have to hurt to be real. That survival isn't the same as peace. That saying yes to someone else should never mean saying no to yourself.

The Found Woman Reflection

Affirmation: *"Love does not require me to abandon myself. I am worthy of ease, affection, and alignment."*

Journal Prompt: What did I believe I had to trade for love—my voice, my dreams, my sense of peace? What parts of myself did I silence in the name of being chosen?

Action Step: Write a letter to your younger self. Tell her everything she needed to hear—what you now know to be true. Speak to her gently, as you would a child. Fold it, seal it, and place it somewhere sacred. Come back to it when you forget your worth.

Devotional: The Woman Who Stayed Too Long

Love that asks you to shrink is not love. Love that requires you to break yourself in half is not love. Love is not a transaction—it's a sanctuary. It's not where you lose yourself, but where you're reminded of who you are.

You don't have to prove your worth by carrying what breaks you. You don't have to stay in places where you're only halfway seen. You are already enough. Your softness, your truth, your presence—it's divine.

Let this be the season where you choose *you*. Not out of bitterness. But out of wholeness. The Found Woman does not beg to be chosen—she remembers she already is.

CHAPTER 3

Becoming the Woman I Didn't Know I Needed

"You can wear the title, play the role, and still feel invisible."

I lost both of my grandmothers within a year, my mother's mother and my father's mother. Two matriarchs. Two pillars. Two women who had helped shape the rhythm of who I was. And with both of them gone, I found myself swallowed by silence. Not just the silence of their absence, but the silence of all the things I hadn't said, hadn't done, hadn't realized until it was too late.

I carried that regret like a weight tucked just beneath my chest. It wasn't dramatic, just ever-present. I wished I had called more. Visited more. Asked them about their youth, their love stories, their pain. I wished I had told them how much I needed them. How much I saw them. But wishing doesn't change the past. It only echoes through your future until you do something different.

Grief is funny like that. It distorts time. It blurs the edges of everything you thought was clear. It slows your thinking, dulls your instincts. And in the haze of loss, I didn't reach for healing. I reached for familiarity.

I reached for him.

Back Into the Fog

He didn't show up for me when I lost them. Not really. Not emotionally. But he was *there*—and in that moment, *being there* felt close enough to love. Grief made me lonely. Vulnerable. Disoriented. I needed someone to hold on to, and instead of standing still to stabilize myself, I moved. I went back. I walked straight into the arms of the man I already knew how to survive.

Before I knew it, we were planning a wedding.

Or rather—I was planning a wedding. He offered assistance here and there, and someone else helped too. But the vision? The organization? The finances? That was all me. Every email sent, every decision made, every flower chosen—it was me holding the pieces together, convincing myself that this was love. Or at least… something like it.

I wasn't excited. Not in the way people expect brides to be. There was no squealing over dresses, no Pinterest boards, no dreamy countdown. Marriage wasn't something I had ever fantasized about. But I did believe in it. I saw it as sacred. A serious, lifelong commitment. I believed that maybe—just maybe—marriage could fix what wasn't working.

I convinced myself that we just needed a fresh start. A new name. A new chapter. I thought the vows would heal us.

But the truth is, nothing changed after we said, "I do."

The Weight of the Ring

We moved into a modest two-bedroom apartment in Baden, Missouri. It wasn't glamorous, but it was ours. And for a little while, things felt stable. Peaceful even. Like an exhale after years of tension. I believed we were finally building something—laying the foundation for a real family.

I walked into the marriage wearing every hat you could imagine: planner, nurturer, peacemaker, cook, maid, co-provider, therapist, "Mrs. Make-It-Happen." I was proud of it at first. I prided myself on being a woman who could do it all, who made a house a home, who showed up.

But slowly… what used to feel like love started to feel like labor.

He stopped saying thank you. Stopped noticing the little things. And I stopped feeling like a partner and started feeling like a convenience. My efforts became expectations. My care became routine. I felt myself disappearing while still moving through all the motions.

And within the first year… infidelity entered our marriage.

It wasn't just the betrayal that broke me—it was the *disillusionment*. The unraveling of everything I thought I knew about love, commitment, and partnership. I had grown up believing that if you gave your all, if you were loyal, if you sacrificed, and prayed, then love would last.

But the lie in that logic is this: love that demands your silence, your self-betrayal, or your suffering—is not love.

The Quiet Shift

The first red flag wasn't the cheating, it was subtle. It was the moment I felt nervous about spending time with certain friends. Like I had to *choose* between keeping him calm and keeping my circle close. That was the whisper. The warning. And when I voiced my discomfort, when I tried to explain how I felt, he told me I was nagging. Dramatic. Ungrateful.

So, I went quiet.

Silence became my survival tactic. I smiled in public and cried in private. I served, cooked, planned, managed, and showed up. But inside, I was vanishing. Emotional neglect turned into emotional manipulation. He may not have hit me, but his words, his absence, left bruises on parts of me I didn't know could bruise.

And still, I stayed.

Because leaving felt like failing. Because I had a son to think about. Because I believed love required sacrifice. Because I wanted to prove I could make it work.

But I was dying inside. Softly. Slowly.

A Soul Ready to Rise

By our tenth wedding anniversary, I felt like I was standing on the edge of myself. Looking over. Wondering who I had become.

That was the moment I began to emotionally detach. I didn't announce it. I didn't pack a bag. But inside… I was already gone.

I started therapy. Quietly. Consistently. It was my secret rebellion against the numbness. Each session peeled back another layer. Each revelation gave me a glimpse of the woman I used to be. The woman I still could become.

I started caring again, about my appearance, my energy, my future. I stood taller. I walked differently. I smiled for *me*. The mirror began to reflect someone I recognized.

Friends started noticing too. Some said something. Others didn't. But I could feel the shift. I wasn't pretending as much at holidays or family gatherings. I wasn't as willing to fake happiness just to keep the peace. The mask was slipping.

And when I finally made the decision to leave—fully leave—I felt a weight lift that I hadn't even realized I'd been carrying.

The Woman in the Mirror

Looking back now, I want to hold her. The version of me who tried so hard to hold it together. Who prayed through pain. Who gave more than she got. Who tried to keep a man, a home, and a heart all intact while hers was breaking silently.

She needed protection.
She needed rest.
She needed truth.

But more than anything, she needed *permission*, to walk away. To choose herself. To believe that love should never cost you your peace, your voice, or your freedom.

I used to think staying made me strong.

Now I know—it was leaving that made me whole.

The Found Woman Reflection

Affirmation: *"I am worthy of love that doesn't require me to disappear to receive it."*

Journal Prompt: What parts of yourself have you silenced in past or current relationships? What would it look like to reclaim those parts today?

Action Step: Create a "Love Inventory." Reflect on what you believed love was then—and what you know love to be now. Identify the gaps and set new standards based on what your healed self deserves.

Devotional: Becoming More Than the Vow

There's a sacredness to commitment, but not all commitments are sacred. Sometimes we cling to vows out of fear, out of duty, or out of hope that love will grow where it's already withered.

You are not bound to brokenness. You are not required to stay in spaces that dim your light. You are allowed to outgrow people, patterns, and promises that no longer serve your healing.

The real vow—the one that matters most—is the one you make to yourself.

To listen deeply. To love fully. To evolve unapologetically. To walk away when staying costs too much.

Be gentle with the version of you who believed struggle was love. She only wanted to be chosen.

And now, you get to choose yourself.

CHAPTER 4

The Shift I Couldn't Unsee

"You can only pretend to be okay for so long before your soul demands more."

The first night I slept alone after leaving my marriage was... strange.

Not freeing. Not tragic. Just strange.

The silence was loud. The space beside me in bed was cold, not just from absence, but from the unfamiliarity of being by myself. I had spent years learning how to coexist, how to anticipate someone else's needs, how to expand or shrink depending on what would keep the peace. Now I was just... me. Alone in a townhome apartment I had chosen. Furnished with what I could afford, filled with unfamiliar quiet. The walls were mine. The peace was mine. But so was the ache.

I stayed at my mom's for about a week right after the separation. She provided a soft landing while I caught my breath, but I knew I couldn't stay there long. I needed a place that was mine, somewhere I could cry freely, heal privately, think clearly. So, I moved into my own place. It was a quiet, necessary kind of rebellion. A declaration: *I'm doing this.*

There came a moment, slow, creeping, but undeniable, when I knew things were off.

At first, it wasn't loud. It was just a yearning. A quiet ache for something deeper, something truer. I craved emotional stability. I wanted to feel desired, not just needed. Protected, not just tolerated. Heard, not just spoken at. Seen, not just as someone's wife or as a mother, but as myself. The full, layered, wild, soft, intuitive, capable, beautiful version of me.

But what I wanted and what I had weren't lining up.

I was showing up, for him, for my child, for our home, but I wasn't being shown up for in return. I found myself shrinking, adapting, pretending. Somewhere along the way, I had stopped showing up for *me*.

I didn't know if what I was longing for was real… or if I was just being unrealistic. Was this just marriage? Was I expecting too much? Was my idea of love and intimacy just a fairy tale I needed to grow out of?

I didn't feel mentally unwell. But looking back now? I was numb.

Not crying. Not fighting. Not dreaming. Just existing.

I was taking muscle relaxers just to sleep, sometimes washing them down with wine. And when I talked to my friends, their stories sounded too similar. It made me wonder if this was just the "normal" everyone tolerated. Everyone seemed to be dealing with some version of disappointment. Everyone seemed to be sacrificing pieces of themselves to say they had someone.

Even therapy didn't help, at least not right away. Vulnerability wasn't something I could access then. I never opened the door to my childhood pain. Never talked about what it meant to have always been the protector. I remember one therapist suggesting my emotional distress came from being unable to conceive again. That wasn't the whole story. I wasn't ready to fix *me*—because I knew even if I did, the environment I was in would never support my healing.

Still, something inside me started waking up.

There wasn't one defining argument that broke me. No grand betrayal. Just the slow, painful erosion of being undone.

So, I started writing.

Not to be petty—but to remember. I had a habit of forgiving too fast. Forgetting too much. Minimizing what hurt me. Writing kept the truth in front of me, even when my heart tried to make excuses. It was a breadcrumb trail back to reality.

I also started walking every day on my lunch break. At first, it was just about air. Then it became about space. Then it became about *me*. Those walks saved me. They were a quiet protest. A way of saying, "I'm still here." A slow reclamation.

And then, one day, I cut my hair.

It wasn't just a style change. It was a shedding. A symbolic release. A declaration that I no longer wanted to carry the weight of pretending. It was one of the first things I did just for me. I looked in the mirror, and for the first time in a long time, I didn't see defeat. I saw *possibility*.

But healing didn't erase the loneliness.

Being without my son during the week felt like losing my shadow. He stayed with his dad to finish the school year, and I got him on weekends. I'd count down to Friday. I'd savor every second. Sunday evenings were always hard. But I had to remind myself, I did this for both of us. I left so we could both be free.

There were moments of guilt. Of second-guessing. Of fear that maybe I had made it all up, maybe things weren't *that* bad. But then I'd remember the silencing. The numbness. The nights I begged God for a sign and still stayed even after the signs came. Those memories kept me grounded.

Friends and family showed up. Some quietly. Some fiercely. My faith? It shifted. I questioned God. I wrestled with Him. I asked "Why?" more times than I could count. I wasn't angry, I was hurt. I thought I had done everything "right." I married the father of my child. I prayed. I stayed. I tried. Why didn't that count?

I didn't have a spiritual routine then. No affirmations, no consistent journaling, no church streak. I was surviving. But I was *aware*. I was watching myself bloom in the dark.

Eventually, I moved into a new apartment in Creve Coeur. And for the first time in a long time… I felt peace.

It wasn't loud. It wasn't dramatic. It was soft, like the settling of dust after a storm. I'd sit in silence and feel grateful for the quiet. I was alone, but I wasn't lonely. I was finally breathing on my own.

I didn't have one "rebirth moment." No grand revelation. No dramatic mirror monologue. My rebirth came in waves. In choosing myself again and again, even when it hurt. Even when it was inconvenient. Even when I didn't know what came next.

Looking back, I'm still proud of her, the woman I was then. She was broken in places, sure. But she was becoming. Quietly, fiercely, and with the kind of strength only pain can teach.

She didn't need someone else to save her.

She was already saving herself.

The Found Woman Reflection

Affirmation: *"I am not hard to love—I was just loving in a place that didn't know how to hold me."*

Journal Prompt: What silent aches have you been carrying? What are the desires you've convinced yourself are "too much"? Where have you been showing up but not being met?

Action Step: Begin a "Truth Journal." Write down things you experience, witness, or feel that your heart keeps trying to forget or dismiss. Let it be your mirror. Let it hold you accountable to your own knowing.

Devotional: A Letter to the One Who's Waking Up

You don't have to wait for permission to change. You don't need someone else to validate your tiredness before you decide to rest. You don't need an outside voice to confirm what your inner whisper has been screaming.

You have a right to desire more. To crave softness and stability. To be loved in ways that feel safe, sacred, and sure. You have a right to return to yourself—even if you're not sure who that is just yet.

This season may not have given you the fairytale you once imagined. But it's giving you something more lasting, *truth*. And truth is the seed of transformation.

Breathe, woman. You are not broken. You are becoming.

CHAPTER 5

The Peace I Chose to Protect

"Peace is not the absence of noise, but the presence of self."

There's a certain stillness that settles over your life—not when everything is perfect, but when you've finally chosen yourself. It doesn't always come with trumpets or some huge awakening. Sometimes, it looks like slipping out of an identity that no longer fits and walking barefoot into uncertainty because your soul needs air.

For me, peace didn't come easy. It came after years of sacrificing my voice, my softness, my joy—for what I thought was love. For what I thought was family. For what I thought I needed to prove.

I realized something had shifted in me when I stopped arguing. I wasn't numb, and I wasn't angry. I was just tired. Tired of begging for the emotional support I gave so freely. Tired of showing up only to be unseen. Tired of wearing the title of "wife" or "friend" like it was the only thing that gave me worth, when in reality, it was choking the very parts of me that were trying to breathe.

I wanted more—emotionally, mentally, spiritually. And I didn't want to feel guilty for craving more anymore.

Creve Coeur: Where Peace Found Me

For the first time in a long time, it didn't just feel like a place to live—it felt like *home*. This new season wrapped itself around me like a warm blanket. It was quiet in the right ways. Soft. Still. Mine.

I started forming new routines. I journaled. I worked out. I prayed. I even got back into therapy. Every small thing I did to reclaim my day-to-day felt like a brick laid on the foundation of a new woman I was building—one choice, one boundary, one breath at a time.

At work, I was thriving. My career gave me something that my personal life hadn't offered in years: stability and confidence. I was in full control of my finances, and with every paycheck, every bill paid, every decision made without needing approval—I felt myself come alive.

There were moments where I would pause in gratitude, just looking around at the life I was creating for myself and my son. I was dressing differently. Dreaming differently. Thinking with clarity. There were no masks to wear. No eggshells to walk on. Just peace. It was quiet, but it was powerful.

My relationship with my son blossomed. It was like us against the world in the best way. He noticed the shift in me too—even if he didn't have the words to describe it. I was showing up for myself, and because of that, I was able to show up for him fully. There was laughter again. Playfulness. Joy. And it felt earned.

But Then… There Was Him.

During this time, I was involved with a man who was married.

It's hard to write. Even harder to admit. But I don't believe in telling half-truths just to sound polished. He filled a void I hadn't yet named. A void that looked like loneliness but ran so much deeper, like the desire to be seen, to be chosen, to be touched in a season where I barely even wanted myself.

We met back in high school. There was always *something* between us, even when nothing was happening. Neither of us were married back then. I married first, and he married years later. But our connection remained. Sometimes it would fade to the background, but it never disappeared.

When I found out my husband had cheated during our first year of marriage, it was him I turned to. Not because I wanted romance, but because I needed someone who could pour into me the way I poured into everyone else. He listened. He encouraged. He reminded me of who I was before life dimmed me. He made me feel safe. Protected. *Seen.*

And eventually, we crossed the line.

We talked every single day. There wasn't a subject off-limits. He knew the parts of me I kept hidden from the world. He visited often, every weekend, sometimes more. I didn't entertain other men. I didn't want to. My heart was already occupied, even if only partially.

He told his wife about me. That made it feel… different. Like it wasn't a secret. Like it wasn't wrong. I told myself it was okay because *I had him first.* Because *she knew.* Because *we understood each other in ways no one else could.*

But guilt doesn't disappear just because it's been justified. There were many nights I prayed, cried, journaled, begged God: "Why can't I leave him alone?" "Why does this feel like love?" "What is broken in me that makes *this* feel like healing?"

And the hardest truth I avoided saying out loud? That we weren't meant to be. That no matter how deep the bond, I would never be his *one.* I would never win the invisible competition I found myself in. I was trying to romanticize a connection born from shared wounds, not shared purpose.

There were many falling outs between us. And during one in particular, the clarity hit hard: I could never be his wife. I could never "trump" her. That realization didn't break me, it freed me.

Detaching from him didn't happen all at once. It was slow. Painful. Familiarity has a way of feeling like home, even when it's hurting you. But I started loosening the grip. I started focusing on the woman I was becoming, not the one who needed someone else to make her feel whole.

I'm still learning. Still shedding. Still rebuilding. But I know now that I deserve a love that is *whole,* not *borrowed.* That I am worthy of being chosen fully, without question, without shame.

The Woman I Was Becoming

In Creve Coeur, something beautiful began. I rediscovered softness. Creativity. My sense of beauty. My goals stretched out in front of me again like open roads. I wasn't afraid to dream anymore. I worked out. I meditated. I learned how to love the silence—not because I was lonely, but because I was whole.
The limiting beliefs I once carried—*that I wasn't smart, beautiful, or capable*—began to unravel. And in their place, new truths took root:
I am *strong.*
I am *intelligent.*
I am *worthy.*
I started building a vision again, real estate, health, entrepreneurship, legacy. I no longer felt like life was something happening to me. I was creating it.

For the Woman in Her Becoming

If you're reading this and see yourself anywhere in my story, whether in the silence, the ache, the entanglement, or the rebirth, I want you to know:
You are not broken.
You are not foolish for loving.
You are not behind.
You are evolving. You are worthy. You are *allowed* to choose yourself—even when it's messy. Even when it hurts. Especially when it hurts.

Peace isn't just something you find. It's something you *protect*.

And *you* are worth protecting.

The Found Woman Reflection

Affirmation:*"I am allowed to choose peace, protect my energy, and grow in stillness. My value is not determined by the noise around me, but by the truth within me."*

Journal Prompt: What does peace look and feel like for you right now? Where in your life have you confused silence with peace, and what truth are you ready to honor instead?

Action Step: Create a "Peace Ritual" for yourself. It could be a walk, journaling for 10 minutes a day, turning off your phone for an hour, or lighting a candle while you breathe deeply. Make peace a practice—not just a concept.

Devotional: The Quiet Power of Peace

Peace isn't something you chase. It's something you create. It's in the boundaries you honor. The decisions you no longer explain. The joy you no longer postpone. The woman you're becoming is not a reaction to pain—but a response to purpose.

When you choose peace, you choose life.

Your own life.

CHAPTER 6

Becoming Her — The Rebirth of the Woman I Buried

"I didn't find her. I became her. The woman who stopped waiting to be chosen and started choosing herself."

For a long time, I thought I had to prove something—to my ex, to the world, maybe even to myself. I wore my survival like a badge of honor. Being strong meant being quiet. Being successful meant holding it all together. Being a woman meant being a wife, a mother, a caretaker… everything to everyone but myself.

But something shifted in me after the divorce. At first, it was subtle. I started to enjoy my own company—really enjoy it. I remembered how full my heart felt in the presence of family. And people began to tell me I seemed different—lighter, more at peace, happy.

One of the most powerful moments of this season was the day I bought my first home. That wasn't just a transaction. It was a triumph. I did that—as a single mom, post-divorce, on my own terms. I did it because I wanted to. That key in my hand? It symbolized the version of me I never thought I'd meet but always hoped existed.

For the first time, I wasn't chasing a role—I was chasing *me*.

It wasn't until after I bought my first home that I truly understood how hollow my achievements had become.

I stood in my new living room—my home, paid for with my own strength, my own name on the deed—surrounded by peace I had fought to create. The floors were mine. The silence was mine. The future was mine.

And yet… something still felt unfinished.

I remember opening my laptop one evening to update my résumé. MBA. Analyst. Supervisor. These were the titles that once gave me a sense of purpose. They were symbols of my ambition, proof that I had "made it"—especially after divorce. I had told myself these accomplishments would validate my worth, protect me from heartbreak, prove I wasn't broken.

But as I sat there, the cursor blinking at me like a silent question mark, I felt… disconnected.

I had built a beautiful life on paper.

But I hadn't yet rebuilt myself.

I had poured so much energy into being productive, being accomplished, being seen as "strong," that I had neglected something more sacred—my softness, my stillness, my soul. I had mistaken being busy for being whole. And I had confused recognition with self-worth.

That night, I realized I didn't need another accolade. I needed alignment.
I didn't want a life that looked good on LinkedIn but felt empty at home.
I didn't want to keep chasing validation when what I truly craved was peace.

For so long, I thought success meant being chosen—by a man, a company, a status. But what I learned, standing in my own home, under my own roof, surrounded by peace I built on my own terms, was this: Being chosen means nothing if you haven't first chosen yourself.

My healing didn't come wrapped in a perfect morning routine. It came through slow, consistent choices. Walks. Music. Yoga. Moments that felt like me reclaiming my body, my joy, and my voice. I started dressing for *myself*. Heels, makeup, all things glam—it wasn't about being seen by others. It was about *seeing me* again.

And oh, how I surprised myself.

There were days I'd catch my reflection and say, "Wow… you did that." I'd feel the shift in my posture, my confidence, my boundaries. I wasn't just existing anymore—I was *living*. Fully. Deeply. Honestly.

If no one else has told you this, let me:
It's okay to start over.
It's okay to let go of identities, dreams, or versions of yourself that no longer serve you.
Starting over isn't failure—it's a repeat with experience.
You were never too much.
You were just pouring into cups that didn't know how to hold your love.

The Found Woman Reflection

Affirmation:*"I choose myself without guilt, and I redefine success on my own terms."*

Journal Prompt: What part of you have you buried beneath roles, relationships, or expectations? What would it look like to let her rise?

Action Step: Take yourself on a solo date this week. Dress up, speak kindly to yourself, and do something that lights *you* up. Afterward, journal about how it felt to show up for *you*.

Found Woman Devotional: "Becoming Her"

No Bible verses. Just truth.

You won't always feel ready.

You won't always feel strong.

But choosing to return to yourself—even when it's unfamiliar—is the holiest act of healing you can offer your soul.

The woman you're becoming isn't waiting to be found.

She's waiting to be *freed*.

She's in the quiet.

She's in the courage.

She's in the mirror.

CHAPTER 7

Soft Doesn't Mean Silent

"Strength doesn't always roar. Sometimes it whispers,
'I choose me.'"

There comes a time when the fight becomes too heavy, not because we are weak, but because we were never meant to carry everything.

I didn't realize how long I had been living in survival mode. My shoulders were always tense. My mind always alert. My voice often quiet in rooms where I should have screamed. I was the woman who held it together. The one who never broke. The one who gave everyone else grace but left none for herself.

It wasn't until years after the divorce, standing in the kitchen with one hand on the stove and the other holding back tears, that I admitted: I am tired.

Tired of fighting to be heard.
Tired of proving I deserved tenderness.
Tired of making a home in places that offered no shelter for my heart.

The Mirror Never Lies

I didn't recognize her anymore, the woman in the mirror.

There was a dullness in her eyes, like someone who'd been standing in the rain for too long without realizing she was soaked. The kind of woman who used to glow now just dimmed herself to fit into spaces that never saw her magic.

And yet, there she was. Still standing.

But standing for what?

I had done everything "right." I wore the right titles. Collected the right degrees. Smiled when expected. Performed strength on cue.

But inside? I was cracking.

I wasn't sure who I was outside of my roles: wife, mother, achiever. I knew how to "do" but not how to be. I could hold down a household, a career, a child—but not myself.

And what's worse? No one knew.

The Slow Softening

The shift didn't happen overnight. There was no dramatic breakdown or movie-worthy scene.

It happened quietly.

In the way I stopped responding to disrespect.
In the way I stopped chasing closure.
In the way I made peace with not being understood.
In the way I started whispering to myself, "I love you. I see you. You're doing great, baby."

Softness began to bloom.

I started lighting candles before bed, not for a man, but for me. I turned off my phone without guilt. I took bubble baths and let the water baptize the woman I was becoming. I played old-school R&B just to sway in the mirror and remember that I was still sensual, still beautiful, still here.

That was my rebellion: coming back to myself.

Redefining Strength & Power

I was learning that true power wasn't about how loud you speak in rooms full of people.

It was how gently you speak to yourself when no one is watching.

And for years, I'd spoken to myself like a drill sergeant.

"You're not doing enough."
"You should've known better."
"Why are you still crying over this?"
"Get up. Push through."

But healing doesn't come through harshness. It comes through tenderness.

So, I changed my language.

I started saying, "You're human."
"You deserve softness too."
"It's okay to rest."
"You don't have to perform worthiness."
"You don't need permission to protect your peace."

Sensuality, Spirit & Soft Power

There was a time when I thought softness meant weakness.
That femininity was about pleasing others.
That sensuality was shameful.
That peace was passive.

But now I know the truth:

Softness is sacred.
Feminine energy is intuitive and protective.
Sensuality is about presence, not performance.
Peace is a boundary, not a byproduct.

Now I sit outside and listen to the wind.
I journal at sunrise with incense curling in the air.
I wear silk robes and speak in soft tones—not because I'm trying to attract anyone, but because I'm honoring me.

And still… I Am Accomplished

Yes, I'm educated.
Yes, I'm capable.
Yes, I'm a provider, a leader, an achiever.

But I'm no longer hiding behind my resume.

Because I remember standing in the home I purchased, barefoot, holding my updated résumé—and realizing it meant nothing if I was emotionally bankrupt.

MBA. Analyst. Supervisor. Realtor. Entrepreneur.
All those titles, and still, I was starving for gentleness.

That day, I let the paper fall to the floor and whispered,
"I want more than this. I want wholeness."

To the Woman Still Hardening to Survive

I see you.

You're tired of being the strong one. You're tired of guarding your softness like it's a liability.

You want to rest. You want to be held. You want to exhale without feeling weak.

Let me say this clearly:

Soft doesn't mean silent.
Soft means safe.
Soft means choosing peace before the storm arrives.
Soft means loving yourself without permission.

You are not too emotional. You are not too sensitive. You are not too much.

You are sacred. You are necessary.

You are allowed to bloom gently.

Softness saved me.

It helped me break the cycle of self-neglect.

It helped me rebuild a relationship with my body, my spirit, and my voice.

It helped me learn how to live—not just exist.

So no, I don't hustle like I used to.

I don't beg for love.

I don't apologize for resting.

Because I am no longer surviving.

I am preserving.

The Found Woman Reflection

Affirmation: *"I release the need to prove. I am soft, sacred, and enough as I am."*

Journal Prompt: In what areas of your life have you confused silence with peace? What does true peace look like for you now?

Action Step: Create a "softness ritual" for your week. Choose one activity that allows you to be fully present, fully you, and commit to doing it without guilt.

Found Woman Devotional: Rest as Resistance

You are not here to hustle your worth. You are not defined by how much you endure. Rest is not laziness. Softness is not weakness. Today, protect your peace like the sacred gift it is. Say no without explanation. Move slowly. Breathe deeply. You do not have to earn ease—you just have to allow it.

CHAPTER 8

When God Whispers, I Listen

"Your spirit always knows before your mind catches up. The whisper doesn't need to be loud to be divine."

The Gut Knows Before the Heart Lets Go

The whispers started long before I had the courage to move. They weren't loud or urgent. They were subtle, soft, barely distinguishable from the noise of daily life. But they were steady. Consistent. Persistent.

"This isn't it."

"You deserve more."

"This is not love."

I ignored those whispers. At first, it was easier to rationalize the familiar than to face the fear of starting over. I told myself things like: "At least he listens sometimes." or "At least he's better than the last one." But comparison isn't clarity. It's compromise.

I stayed with the married man longer than I should have, not because I didn't hear the truth, but because I didn't want to accept it. I convinced myself that because we had history, we had a future. That because he was emotionally present in ways my ex-husband never was, it meant something deeper.

But love isn't love if it makes you question your worth.

He made me feel like my emotions were excessive, like my desire to be fully chosen was unreasonable. And so, I started questioning myself instead of the situation. That's what happens when you ignore your gut—you turn down your own volume.

When Religion Wasn't Enough

People saw the polished version of me. The girl who smiled. The woman who still went to church. The single mother holding it all together. But what they didn't see was the unraveling happening behind closed doors.

They didn't see the mornings I sat in my car outside my job, frozen, unsure if I could face the day.

They didn't see the nights I cried into pillows, asking God if I was unlovable, broken, or being punished.

And the truth? I had grown tired of church.

Not tired of God, but tired of the version of God I was handed.

The sermons no longer nourished me. The scriptures felt rehearsed. I wanted something deeper, something ancestral, something that made sense of both my pain and my power. I couldn't reconcile a God of love with generational oppression. I couldn't find healing in a space that didn't hold the complexity of being Black, woman, and wounded.

So, I searched.

I read about African spirituality. I lit candles not just in ritual, but in remembrance. I started speaking to my ancestors, feeling them near when I was alone. I began to understand that divinity isn't confined to a pulpit or a pew.

God, for me, was in the wind. In the silence. In the mirror.

And yes, God was still in my tears.

Silent Endings, Sacred Boundaries

Letting go of friends I'd known since my teenage years? That part nearly broke me.

These were women who knew my secrets, my childhood crushes, my pregnancies, my heartbreaks. We had history. Loyalty. Codependency. But over time, I started to feel the imbalance. I'd show up for birthdays, support their dreams, answer every "Can I vent?" phone call, and yet, when I needed support? Silence.

There were snide remarks disguised as jokes. Control masked as concern. Envy hiding behind shallow compliments. I tried to speak on it. I tried to salvage it.

But not all friendships are meant to last forever.

Some are only meant to teach you how to love yourself better.

So, I exited quietly, not in anger, but in reverence for my own peace. That was hard for someone like me. I was raised on loyalty. I clung to it like breath. But the truth is, loyalty without reciprocity is self-abandonment.

Silence became my boundary. And peace became my inheritance.

When My Inner Voice Got Louder

There was a time when I needed others to co-sign every decision. I needed reassurance that I was doing the right thing. But now? I sit in silence, and I listen.

To my gut.

To God.

To the little girl inside me.

To the ancestors who whisper, "Keep going, baby, we survived so you could bloom."

That voice I used to drown out with distractions is now the one I trust most. It doesn't yell. It never pressures. But it doesn't lie.

It tells me when to leave, when to rest, when to speak up, and when to let go.

It tells me when I'm self-sabotaging. When I'm playing small. When I'm betraying myself for comfort.

And I listen now. Every time.

A Sacred Return

I no longer need grand signs to know when something is off. I don't need lightning bolts or loud breakups. I just need that whisper— that knowing.

Because now I know:
Peace is a compass.
Repetition is a red flag.
My intuition is holy.
God doesn't yell. God whispers.
And when God whispers, I listen.

This chapter taught me that evolution isn't loud. It's soft. It happens in silence. It unfolds in the quiet corners of your heart when no one else is watching.

To the woman still afraid of leaving what's comfortable: You already know what to do. Your body knows. Your soul knows. The whisper has already spoken.

Your only job is to listen—and obey.

The Found Woman Reflection

Affirmation: *"My voice is sacred, and I trust the whispers within. Even when the world is loud, I will listen to the stillness of my spirit. I am deeply aligned with my inner knowing."*

Journal Prompt: When was the last time your spirit tried to speak, but you ignored it?

What did you fear, and what do you know now?

Action Step: Identify one small area in your life where you've been ignoring your intuition.

Take one action today that aligns with what your inner voice has been trying to say.

Found Woman Devotional: Whispers Over Thunder

There was a time when I thought God had to come through thunderclaps, miracles, or someone else's voice. I thought wisdom had to sound like a sermon. But now I know better. Sometimes, the divine comes through a whisper—a nudge you feel in your stomach. A tug at your spirit. A voice that sounds like your own, but more ancient, more whole.

That voice doesn't rush or yell. It waits. It nudges. It invites you to choose yourself.

So, when God whispers, I no longer talk over it.

I get quiet. I lean in. I listen.

CHAPTER 9

Becoming the Woman I Prayed For

"I didn't just survive—I became her. The woman I once whispered about in my prayers is now the woman I greet in the mirror."

There was a time when I thought "becoming her" meant perfecting myself. If I could just fix the flaws, lose the weight, say the right things, make the right moves—maybe I'd finally *feel* like her. That strong, radiant, fulfilled version of me. The one who didn't second-guess, who wasn't burdened by the past, who glowed from the inside out.

But I didn't become her in the spotlight.

I met her in the shadows.

I met her in moments of silence—where my thoughts were loud and my heart was aching. I met her in the mirror, face swollen from crying, eyes searching for peace. I met her when I walked away from what I thought I wanted. I met her in the middle of anxiety attacks, silent prayers, and empty bank accounts. And each time I chose to show up, she rose a little more.

Becoming the woman I prayed for wasn't a straight line.

It was a spiral.

I kept circling back to old patterns, old fears, old doubts—but each time, I returned with more awareness. More grace. More truth.

The Power of Reclamation

She didn't just arrive one day. I had to reclaim her.

Piece by piece.

I had to reclaim my **voice**—the one I muted to make others comfortable.

My **body**—the one I criticized, hid, and overworked.

My **dreams**—the ones I buried because someone else couldn't see the vision.

My **self-worth**—the one I confused with validation, money, or performance.

It wasn't a magical transformation. It was slow. Sacred. Unfolding. Some days, I felt like I was blossoming. Other days, like I was breaking.

But even in the breaking, something beautiful was happening: I was no longer abandoning myself.

I stopped waiting for permission.

I stopped over-apologizing.

I stopped silencing my truth to maintain someone else's peace.

The Battle Between Who I Was and Who I Was Becoming

There's a tension that lives in transformation.

The old you clings to comfort.

The new you whispers, "You don't live there anymore."

There were days I missed the version of me who didn't know better—because she didn't feel all this pain. But I also realized she didn't know this power.

I outgrew relationships I once begged God to fix.

I outgrew careers I once thought defined me.

I even outgrew parts of my identity I thought were permanent.

I became more honest. More discerning. More tender.

And I learned that being the woman I prayed for isn't about having it all together.

It's about trusting myself—especially when everything feels uncertain.

It's about choosing peace, not perfection.

It's about living with integrity, not performance.

A Return, Not a Reinvention

I used to think I was becoming someone new.

But the truth is—I was returning to someone ancient.

The woman I prayed for is the woman I've always been.

Before heartbreak.

Before people-pleasing.

Before survival mode.

She was waiting for me to come home.

And now that I'm here, I protect her differently.

I guard my peace.

I honor my "no."

I rest without guilt.

I receive without fear.

I no longer shrink to be chosen.

I no longer perform to be seen.

I no longer overgive to feel worthy.

I am the woman I prayed for—because I learned how to pray with my actions.

Not just with my words.

The Found Woman Reflection

Affirmation: *"I am no longer who I used to be—and that is sacred. I honor my evolution, even when it's slow. I trust the woman I am becoming."*

Journal Prompt: What does the "healed" version of you look and feel like?

Where are you still resisting her?

What would happen if you stopped trying to become her and simply allowed her to *be*?

Action Step: Choose one ritual that aligns with the woman you're becoming—whether it's waking up early, drinking water with intention, saying "no" without explanation, or speaking kindly to yourself—and do it daily for the next 7 days.

Found Woman Devotional: "God, Thank You for Her."

God, thank you for the woman I am becoming.

Not the polished version, not the one that others expect—but the whole version.

The one who fought her way here, who listened even when she was afraid,

who let go of what wasn't hers so she could make space for what was.

Thank you for the wisdom that came through waiting.

Thank you for the strength that bloomed in surrender.

Thank you for the peace that no longer needs to be earned—but is now embodied.

And thank you for reminding me that I never had to become someone else.

I only had to come home… to me.

CHAPTER 10

Healing the Father Wound

"She stopped looking for her father in men the moment she became the woman she needed as a child."

There's a particular ache that lingers when your first love— your father—teaches you to question your worth through absence, inconsistency, or emotional silence. It's not always loud. Sometimes, it's the quiet ache in your chest when no one notices you. Sometimes, it's the hyper-independence you wear like armor. And sometimes, it's in the relationships you choose— chasing pieces of the man who never gave you all of him.

The Man I First Knew

My father was playful. He was the one who cracked jokes in the kitchen and made meals on his good days. He was the lenient one. The one we could get a "yes" from. But there was another side— one where shadows often took over. He would isolate. He became irritable, emotionally distant. He fought demons we couldn't see but could feel.

I lived with both of my parents, but emotional proximity doesn't always come with physical presence. There's a difference between a man being in the house and being in your life.

One of the most painful memories I carry is the day my sister begged him to come home. The way she cried. The way we waited. And the way his shame kept him away from us. I still remember the picture of my older sister on his dashboard. Just her. Not me. Not my younger sister. That photo whispered what my mouth couldn't say at the time: *You are not seen.*

Invisible, But Not Broken

I don't know when exactly I started trying to prove I was worthy. I just remember always trying to be "good." To not cause waves. To be the strong one. Somewhere along the line, I became the girl who didn't cry too much, didn't ask for too much, didn't expect too much. Because if I didn't expect, I couldn't be let down.

But the wound didn't disappear. It just showed up in different ways.

Loving in His Image

I didn't realize until after my divorce that the men I loved mirrored my father in so many ways. Emotionally unavailable. Gentle in appearance but absent in presence. My husband was him in different clothes. The way he showed up—then withdrew. The way I begged to be noticed without using words.

Still, each man I chose gave me *something* my father didn't. Maybe it was attention. Maybe it was desire. But it was never safety. I didn't know how to receive that anyway. I was too used to *providing* it.

I don't know the exact moment when I knew something had to change. Maybe it was when I realized how I handled him—emotionally, mentally, spiritually—compared to how he handled me. The imbalance became too loud to ignore.

The Journey to Unlearning

My healing didn't come overnight. It came in layers—through therapy, journaling, solitude, and motherhood. Each process peeled back a version of me who had only known how to love in survival mode.

I've never felt like I needed his *approval.* But I needed his love. His protection. I needed to feel like someone would choose me without hesitation. I needed him to say, "You're safe now. I've got you." Since he couldn't, I had to learn to say it to myself.

Now, when the little girl in me cries out, I answer. I remind her: *You are safe. You are seen. I've got you now.*

Understanding the Man, Releasing the Grip

I don't know if I've fully forgiven him, but I understand him now. I see his humanity. I know he did the best he could with what he knew. I know he didn't have the tools, and that doesn't make the wound disappear—but it does soften it.

This healing has reshaped the way I love others. I love hard. Through action. Through loyalty. But I'm still guarded when it comes to being loved. That's my next layer to peel.

And maybe, just maybe, becoming the woman, I needed all along is enough. Maybe that's how I heal us both.

The Found Woman Reflection

Affirmation: *"I release the need to be chosen by the one who couldn't see me. I am already worthy of love, safety, and devotion."*

Journal Prompt: When was the first time you felt emotionally unseen or unsafe by your father—or a father figure? How did that moment shape the way you love or expect love?

Action Step: Write a letter to your younger self—specifically the version of you who felt invisible. Tell her what she needed to hear then. Fold it, place it somewhere sacred, and return to it when the wound resurfaces.

Found Woman Devotional: "God, Teach Me to Receive"

God, I've learned how to love deeply.

I've learned how to pour out, show up, and carry more than I was ever meant to hold.
But now I'm learning the sacred art of receiving.

Receiving love that doesn't require exhaustion.
Receiving peace that isn't earned.
Receiving safety without proving I deserve it.

I release the belief that love must hurt.
I surrender the fear that says I am too much—or not enough.

Let me be soft without shrinking.
Let me trust love again, without betraying myself.
Let me rest in the truth that I am worthy—not because of what I do, but because of who I am.

Teach me to receive love that mirrors the healing I've worked for.
Let the next love be peace. Let the next love be home.

Amen.

CHAPTER 11

Love After Lessons

"Real love doesn't demand the performance of pain. It
invites you to rest, be seen, and be safe."

T here was a time I believed love was measured by sacrifice.
How much I could endure.
How much I could give.
How long I could stay when it stopped feeling like home.

I didn't know that I had been taught to equate love with struggle. That consistency didn't mean peace—it meant availability. That affection didn't mean alignment—it just meant presence. I didn't know how to discern devotion from codependency, or passion from trauma bonding. Because I thought love had to be earned.

I didn't know that real love doesn't come from shrinking yourself to fit someone else's comfort. It doesn't demand silence, or apologies for being too emotional, too soft, too vocal, too much. Real love doesn't see you as a burden—it treats you like a blessing.

But I had to live through what love wasn't before I could ever receive what love truly is.

The Lessons Love Taught Me Through Pain

I once thought love had to be proven through labor—constant texting, long conversations, emotional contortions to be enough. If he didn't check in, my worth wavered. If he grew distant, I clung tighter. I didn't know that I was building intimacy on fear, not truth.

I saw red flags and called them potential.
I watched love become a performance.

And I played my part well.

Smiling. Showing up. Staying quiet when it hurt.

Because I thought loyalty was louder than logic.

I confused attention for affection. Control for care.

And when it ended, I thought it was my fault for not doing more. Being more.

But the truth? That kind of love was never real. It was survival. And survival isn't sustainable.

The Shift: From Hustling to Healing

The turning point didn't come in one explosive moment. It came in whispers—like so much of growth does.

- In the silence of being alone and not feeling lonely.
- In the warmth of my own presence.
- In the clarity that followed solitude.

I started asking myself different questions.

Not "Does he like me?"

But "Do I like how I feel around him?"

Not "How can I keep him?"

But "Does this version of me even want to stay?"

And most importantly: "Is this love making me softer—or harder?"

Because real love should soften you. Not bruise your spirit.

Rewriting the Story: What Love Looks Like Now

Today, love is no longer about proving anything.

It's about ease.

It's about breath.

It's about being able to exhale in someone's presence and still feel held.

Love now feels like:

- Eye contact that lingers without possession.

- Touch that heals without expectation.
- Words that affirm, not confuse.
- Space that feels safe, not silent.

It's a text message that doesn't leave you anxious.
It's a conversation that leaves you fuller.
It's someone showing up—not just when it's convenient, but because they choose to. Over and over again.

The Power of Choosing Me First

I used to pray for someone to choose me.
Now I thank God that I chose myself first.
That I decided peace was non-negotiable.
That I released relationships where love felt like labor.
That I stopped asking for the bare minimum and started expecting more—not from others, but from myself.
I am no longer available for half-love.
No longer performing for proximity.
No longer entertaining men who don't know how to handle the fullness of a healed, whole woman.

Love That Matches My Evolution

The love I desire now is rooted in respect, peace, and spiritual alignment.
It's someone who:

- Honors my boundaries, not challenges them.
- Recognizes my strength, but nurtures my softness.
- Listens when I speak, not just hears.
- Loves my mind, my body, and my spirit—in harmony.

It's not about perfection.
It's about partnership.
It's not always loud, but it is always felt.

To the Woman Reading This…

If you're in a season where love feels confusing—pause.
Ask yourself if you're chasing peace or familiarity.
Ask yourself if you're being held or just tolerated.
Ask yourself if you're being watered or slowly wilting.
The woman you're becoming cannot afford to stay where she's not growing.
And I promise, there is love that won't ask you to bleed to prove you're worthy of being held.
There is love that will meet you in your softness and say, "Stay as you are—I've got you."
But that love won't arrive until you stop settling for the kind that leaves you questioning your reflection.

Love Is a Mirror

Now, I use love as a mirror.
If I feel anxious, I check my peace.
If I feel confused, I check my boundaries.
If I feel small, I check my alignment.
Because I've learned: love isn't supposed to hurt.
It's not supposed to leave you doubting your worth.
It's supposed to feel like coming home—to yourself, and to another.
And I am home now.
Finally.
To myself.
To love.
To peace.

The Found Woman Reflection

Affirmation: *"I no longer chase love. I attract what aligns with my peace, honors my worth, and welcomes my softness."*

Journal Prompt: Where in my life am I still performing for love instead of simply receiving it? How can I shift to a space of resting in love?

Action Step: List the three most important boundaries you've created around love. Reaffirm them out loud to yourself today. Post them on your mirror, or make them a lock screen reminder.

Found Woman Devotional: "Love is Not a Reward"

Love is not something to earn—it is something to receive.

You don't have to shrink, perform, or prove yourself to be held in real love. You don't have to "get it all right" to be loved in a way that feels like home. Love that honors your spirit will never feel like pressure. It will feel like peace.

Take time today to speak lovingly to yourself. To honor your softness. To welcome the version of you that no longer needs to be rescued—but still deserves to be cherished.

You are worthy of a love that mirrors the love you've cultivated within yourself.

CHAPTER 12

The Found Woman Within

"She went searching for love, security, and success—only to find herself."

There comes a time when you stop running. Not because the race is over, but because you finally realize you were never chasing the right finish line to begin with.

For so long, I was in pursuit of being "enough." Enough for the man I married. Enough for my family. Enough for the church. Enough for the world. Enough for the married man. Enough for the version of my father I never truly had. I thought if I could just succeed—climb the ladder, look the part, play the role—then maybe I'd finally be validated. Seen. Loved. Safe.

But in becoming what I thought others needed, I was slowly disappearing.

Piece by piece, my voice, my softness, my truth, my dreams—they all faded. I was performing strength, wearing success like armor. I had the degrees, the job titles, the home. But deep down, I was still the little girl hoping someone would choose her first. Hoping to hear "I'm proud of you." Hoping for protection and presence that never came in the ways I needed it.

The Root of the Void

What I now understand is that my lifelong search for love—for partnership, for approval, for belonging—wasn't just about romance. It was about the **void left by a father wound**. The absence didn't always look like absence; sometimes, it looked like inconsistency, like emotional unavailability, like wanting to be enough but never quite feeling it.

I looked for him in other people. In men who were unavailable. In friends I overextended myself for. In jobs I overworked in. I didn't know how to just "be"—because I was conditioned to earn my place in people's lives. To hustle for affection. To audition for worth.

But you can't earn what should've been freely given.

I had to mourn the fantasy of the father I wished for, so I could stop making broken choices from a place of longing. That mourning was sacred. It allowed me to reparent myself, to become the safe space I had always craved. It allowed me to say: *You didn't deserve that absence. But you do deserve healing.*

The Day I Returned to Myself

The woman I am today is unapologetic, authentic, free, and beautiful—not because life has been easy, but because I finally gave myself permission to be whole. I had to reclaim my voice—the one I silenced to keep the peace. I had to realign my dreams—the ones I buried beneath everyone else's expectations. I forgave the version of me who didn't know better. And now, I plan my future based on goals that are deeply personal, not performative.

I no longer need to perform for the mirror.

There was a day I stood in that mirror, looked myself in the eyes, and whispered: *You are the love you've been waiting for. You're no longer the woman begging to be seen. You are the one who sees herself now.* That was the moment I became my own witness.

A Rebirth in Spirit

My spiritual lens shifted in this season—not just in practice, but in power. I moved from a rigid, performative faith to a softer, sacred connection with the Divine. I began to see God not as a judge, but as a presence. The more I connected with nature, with silence, and with my own body—the more I remembered that I was never broken. I was simply buried. Under grief. Under duty. Under doubt.

I started lighting candles not just for ambiance, but for clarity. I stopped begging God to change people and started asking God to reveal me to myself. I started calling on ancestors for strength. I stopped being afraid to feel beautiful. To feel powerful. To feel divine.

And in that remembering—I found my way back to her.

Living As a Found Woman

To be a Found Woman is to finally realize that everything you searched for was waiting inside of you the whole time. It's not a final destination—it's a divine remembrance. It's coming home to the parts of yourself you once thought you had to give away to be loved.

Now I live by the truth that my inner voice is sacred. That being seen by others starts with seeing myself. That being loved well starts with loving myself first.

If I could speak to the version of me that still equated abandonment with unworthiness, I would wrap her in the kind of hug she always deserved. I'd tell her: *You were never too much. You were never hard to love. You were just waiting to be loved correctly.*

And now, I love her well. Fully. Loudly. Softly. Consistently.

This Is Legacy

As I carry this legacy—not just for myself, but for my son, for the women who watch me, for the little girl who still lives inside me— I do so with deep intention. I want my son to see what it means to build something rooted in truth, not performance. I want women to feel inspired not just to tap into their femininity—but to live there. To honor their softness. To own their power. To rise with elegance. To speak with fire. To rest without guilt.

Legacy is not just what we leave behind. It's what we embody while we're here.

And I?

I am the embodiment of the woman I prayed to become.

I am her.

Finally.

The Found Woman Reflection

Affirmation: *"I am no longer lost in other people's expectations. I am found in my truth, my voice, and my power."*

Journal Prompt: Write a letter to your younger self. What do you want her to know about who you've become?

Action Step: Spend time this week doing something that your past self never thought she deserved—whether that's rest, joy, softness, or silence. Let it be a celebration of the woman you've reclaimed.

Found Woman Devotional: "Come Home to Yourself"

There is a sacred home inside you. A place where shame has no keys. Where dreams are welcome. Where peace pours into every crack the world once broke open. This is the place where your truth lives—soft, whole, radiant.

To come home to yourself is not to be perfect. It is to be present. Not to be without flaw—but to love yourself **with full awareness** of every layer. To return to your body, your voice, your rhythm—without apology.

Let this chapter be a reminder: You are not behind. You are not broken. You are **becoming**. And everything you need is already within.

CHAPTER 13

The Legacy I'm Living

"She didn't just rebuild her life—she redefined what legacy means."

There's a power that comes when you realize you're not just surviving anymore—you're leading.

Not leading in the corporate sense. Not just managing a home or guiding a child. But leading with your life.

Your joy becomes resistance. Your healing becomes generational. Your softness becomes strategy. Your presence becomes purpose.

Mothering From Wholeness

Being a mother changed me—but healing changed how I mother.

I used to think my role was to give my son the life I didn't have. I wanted him to never feel the voids I carried for so long—voids I masked with achievements, relationships, and responsibilities. But now I understand—my greatest gift to him is becoming the woman I was always meant to be.

A woman who loves herself, speaks life into her future, and walks in peace—not pressure.
My son doesn't need a perfect mother. He needs a present one. He needs to see what resilience looks like without self-neglect. What boundaries look like without bitterness. What softness looks like without shame.

When I bought our first home—post-divorce, single, with just faith, spreadsheets, and divine timing—it wasn't just about shelter. It was sacred. A tangible declaration that I could build again. That I could be the matriarch of my own story. That I didn't need permission—I only needed vision.

I want him to see that legacy isn't just in land or money. It's in character. In healing. In peace. In joy. In choosing yourself boldly so others can learn how to do the same.

Sisterhood, Redefined

Healing also changed how I show up in friendships. For years, I held on to relationships that no longer poured into me—friends I defended during my marriage, stood by in tough times, and loved deeply. But love without reciprocity is exhausting. I realized I was over-showing up for people who wouldn't even show up for themselves, let alone for me.

It was hard to accept that longevity doesn't guarantee loyalty. That sometimes the people who walk with you the longest can still misunderstand the woman you're becoming.

But walking away wasn't about anger. It was about alignment.

True sisterhood feels safe. It doesn't require performance. It holds space when you're broken and celebrates loudly when you're whole. I found new sisters in unexpected places—women who weren't threatened by my glow but reflected it.

I learned that sisterhood starts within. The way you treat yourself will always echo in your relationships. And I vowed that I would never again stay in spaces where I had to shrink in order to be accepted.

Money, Mastery & Self-Worth

Let's talk about money—not just the currency, but what it represents.

There was a time I equated my worth to the size of my paycheck, the number of degrees I held, the grind in my schedule. The busier

I was, the more "valuable" I felt. But healing forced me to sit still. To ask: Who are you when the hustle stops?

And that's when I discovered wealth was never about accumulation—it was about alignment.

Now, I believe financial growth is just one part of holistic success. I want freedom—not just funds. Peace—not just promotions. I want to live well, not just work hard.

I began shifting my mindset:

- No more scarcity thinking.
- No more guilt around desiring luxury.
- No more minimizing my needs to make others comfortable.

Now I invest in things that feed my future: therapy, rest, education, assets, boundaries, and sacred opportunities. I no longer live by the numbers— live by the impact.

I want to leave my son more than money—I want to leave him a model. A model of how to earn without losing yourself. How to build without burning out. How to love without losing your identity. How to dream audaciously without dimming your light.

Healing the Root: The Father Wound

And if I'm being honest, much of what I've had to unlearn traces back to the relationship I never had—a father who wasn't emotionally available, present, or prepared to affirm a daughter like me.

My "daddy issues" weren't just about him. They were about the way I searched for him in men, in mentors, in moments where I just wanted someone to say, "You're enough as you are."

I craved safety in masculine energy because I had never fully received it. So, I confused control with care. Possessiveness with protection. And attention with love.

That unhealed space in me kept choosing men who mirrored the same emotional distance I grew up around. I kept trying to earn love instead of simply receiving it. But the little girl in me deserved more. She deserved safety, consistency, and softness.

So, I reparented her. I listened to her. I stopped abandoning her in pursuit of being chosen. And I made a vow—to no longer outsource my worth.

That's part of my legacy, too: breaking that cycle. Being the love I needed. So that my son doesn't have to question his value. So that he knows how to give and receive love that is whole, healthy, and healing.

Legacy, Redefined

To me, legacy isn't just a last name or what's written in a will. It's how your presence lingers after you leave the room. It's the permission you give others to rise, to rest, to return to themselves.

I'm not building from pain anymore. I'm building from purpose.

And every decision I make now—from business to motherhood to love—is rooted in that truth:
I am the legacy.

The Found Woman Reflection

Affirmation: *"My legacy is alive in how I love, how I lead, and how I live."*

Journal Prompt: What does legacy mean to you—outside of money? What do you want your children, family, or community to feel when they remember you?

Action Step: Take one step this week that plants a seed for your legacy—whether it's opening a savings account, setting a boundary, having a hard conversation, or writing your vision down.

Found Woman Devotional: "You Are the Root and the Bloom"

There is a lineage inside you—rich, resilient, radiant.

Your ancestors dreamed of a day when you'd have the freedom to choose softness over struggle. Rest over rushing. Power over proving. You are both their wildest dream *and* your own sacred creation.

Legacy isn't just what you leave behind—it's how you live right now. Every choice you make in love, money, motherhood, or sisterhood—carries energy forward. You are the garden and the gardener. The seed and the soil. The root and the bloom.

And you, Found Woman, are flourishing.

CHAPTER 14

Becoming Her, Again and Again

"Every time I chose myself, I met a new version of me."

There's a moment in every woman's life when she realizes: She is no longer becoming who others expect. She is becoming herself. Not the version shaped by pain. Not the one built on performance or perfection. But the woman beneath it all—raw, radiant, resilient.

Cycles, Seasons, and Sacred Becoming

Healing isn't linear. Growth isn't a straight line. There were days I felt like I was thriving—and others where I was just surviving. There were seasons of joy, followed by shadows of doubt. And yet, in each cycle, I found pieces of myself I didn't know were missing.

I stopped asking, "When will I finally be whole?" and instead whispered, "What part of me is emerging now?" That shift changed everything. It gave me grace for the process. It gave me peace in the pauses. It allowed me to love the in-between, not just the breakthroughs.

I learned that I don't have to be constantly evolving to be worthy. I can rest and still be becoming. I can break and still be beautiful. I can sit still and still be growing. That was the sacred revelation— the power of not just surviving change but allowing it to birth something softer, more divine in me.

Embracing the Becoming

The Found Woman isn't a destination. She's a movement. A rhythm. A lifestyle. She learns. She sheds. She evolves. She rises.

Over and over and over again. She isn't defined by her worst decisions—or her best days. She is defined by her ability to return to herself every time she drifts.

In this version of me, I don't need permission to be soft. I don't need applause to feel validated. I don't need love that comes with conditions. I've become the love I need. The peace I seek. The woman I once dreamed of.

But becoming her didn't come without cost. There were tears I never admitted, questions I never voiced, and heartbreaks I tried to heal in silence. There were days when I questioned if I would ever feel joy again. But each time I returned to myself, I remembered: I am my safest place.

I found that stillness didn't mean stagnation. It meant I was finally listening. Listening to my body, my spirit, my needs. I learned to stop abandoning myself for temporary comfort. I learned to stop betraying my truth to keep false peace. I learned that growth often looks like solitude before it looks like celebration.

An Open Invitation

To every woman reading this: You don't have to wait until everything is perfect to begin again. You don't need a map to come home to yourself. You just need a whisper. A nudge. A tiny belief that maybe, just maybe, there's more for you. And guess what? There is.

You don't need to be "ready." You just need to be willing. To release. To remember. To return to the woman you were always meant to be.

She is not behind you. She is within you. And every time you choose yourself, you breathe life into her. Again and again.

The Power of Solitude, Singleness & Silence

For so long, I feared being alone. I thought solitude meant something was wrong with me—that if no one was choosing me, I must not be worthy. But what I've come to learn is that sacred solitude is where the most powerful transformation happens.

Aloneness taught me that I wasn't as polished as I thought. That beneath the performing and pretending was a woman craving peace. A woman who needed to stop striving long enough to hear herself.

There's a difference between loneliness and sacred solitude. Loneliness is when you're too broken to sit with yourself. Sacred solitude is a comforting place because you accept your brokenness and allow God and the universe to speak to you and guide you in doing the work.

In silence, I learned that my overthinking wasn't always wisdom—it was fear. That my second-guessing was a product of trauma, not truth. I realized I wasn't broken. I was simply buried under expectations that were never mine to carry.

Every version of me was worthy. Even the confused one. Even the one who didn't know how to receive it. Even the one who cried herself to sleep. Each of them helped birth the woman I am today.

So, to you, sister—if you're standing in the mirror wondering when you'll feel whole again, this is your reminder: you're already on your way. Every quiet morning, every boundary held, every tear released in private is a step closer to becoming her.

Not once. Not twice. But again and again.

With every return to yourself, you reclaim your power.

The Found Woman Reflection

Affirmation: *"I am a masterpiece in motion. Becoming is my birthright."*

Journal Prompt: What version of yourself are you being invited to become in this season? What would it look like to meet her with curiosity, not judgment?

Action Step: Create a *Becoming List*: Write down five qualities, habits, or beliefs you want to embody in this next chapter. Then take one small step toward one of them this week.

Found Woman Devotional: "You Are Still Becoming"

You are not late. You are not behind. You are not broken.

You are in bloom. In motion. In sacred transformation.

And every version of you—every cracked-open, wild-hearted, breath-held-through-the-hard-seasons version—matters. Every layer. Every fall. Every rise.

So, walk boldly. Love deeply. Reflect often. And know that you can always return to the path of becoming.

Because **being found** doesn't mean you're done growing. It means you finally know the way back to yourself.

CHAPTER 15

Rewriting My Money Story

"I thought money would make me feel worthy—until I learned my worth was never for sale."

The Currency of Worth

I didn't grow up with a solid understanding of money. It wasn't openly discussed at home. We weren't taught to save, budget, or build—we were taught to stretch, survive, and make do. Even when I took a financial literacy course in high school, the lessons were absorbed just long enough to pass the class. I'd later spend years in the banking industry, ironically helping others manage their finances while never fully applying those tools to my own life.

And for a while, I didn't think it mattered. I equated financial peace with income. As long as the check cleared, I was okay. But what I didn't realize was that behind every overdraft, every impulse purchase, every period of feast and famine, there was something deeper at play—*my self-worth*.

Survival Mode Spending

When I had money, I spent to feel something—joy, validation, relief. When I didn't have money, I felt shame, anxiety, and defeat. The fluctuations weren't just in my bank account—they were in my identity. Money became a mirror, reflecting how I felt about myself. And during the lowest points—job loss, income drops, emotional burnout—it felt like I was failing not just financially, but personally.

There were seasons where I made more than enough, but the fear of not having lingered. I'd overspend trying to prove I was "doing okay," even if I wasn't. Then came the spiral: the guilt, the secrecy, the silence. Financial trauma isn't always about poverty—it's about the emotional weight we tie to money. The scarcity mindset, the belief that stability is temporary, the subconscious fear that it will all disappear. I knew it too well.

The Shame We Don't Talk About

No one tells you how hard it is to rebuild after financial shame. To admit you knew better but still fell behind. To have the degrees, the job titles, and still feel like you're drowning. We don't talk enough about how money wounds the soul—not just the wallet. The pressure to appear put together when inside, you're unraveling.

And as a Black woman, the expectations were louder. Be strong. Be successful. Don't ask for help. Don't show weakness. I wore the mask and paid the price. Emotionally. Mentally. Financially.

A New Definition of Wealth

Healing my relationship with money didn't happen overnight. It came through small choices:

- Saying no to overextending myself to "look" successful.
- Choosing to rest instead of hustle when I was burnt out.
- Creating budgets that prioritized peace, not pressure.
- Investing in therapy instead of temporary distractions.
- Learning that financial freedom also meant emotional freedom.

I no longer define wealth by numbers alone. My richest moments have been in stillness, not in spending. Peace, not possessions. Clarity, not consumption.

Now, I move with intention. I forgive my past choices, honor the lessons, and choose a future where my self-worth isn't tied to my bank account. I am building not just assets—but alignment. I want my son to inherit more than money. I want him to inherit *wisdom*. A model of how to thrive without sacrificing himself in the process.

The Found Woman Reflection

Affirmation: *"My worth is not measured by my income, but by the truth of who I am. I release shame and choose financial peace."*

Journal Prompt:
- In what ways have I tied my value to money or success?
- What old beliefs about money no longer serve me—and what new truths am I ready to embrace?

Action Step: Create a financial peace plan—not just a budget. Write down three ways you can bring calm to your financial life this week, whether it's reviewing your subscriptions, setting a savings goal, or journaling after each spending decision.

Found Woman Devotional: "God, Let Me Live Rich in Soul First"

God, I used to chase abundance as if it lived outside of me—in numbers, in achievements, in the eyes of others.
But now I know: true wealth starts within.

Let my heart be rich in peace.
Let my days overflow with meaning.
Let my relationships echo wholeness—not hustle.

I release every story that said I had to earn my worth.
I let go of the fear that if I stop striving, I'll lose everything.
I welcome the wisdom that money is not my master—it's my mirror.
A reflection of how deeply I trust myself, and You.

Teach me to build from alignment, not anxiety.

To attract from overflow, not obligation.
To let stillness speak louder than scarcity.

I am already in abundance.
And everything I need flows from there.

Amen.

CHAPTER 16

The Stillness That Saved Me

"In the silence, I finally heard my soul speak."

There was a time when stillness felt like suffocation.
Like punishment.
Like failure.

I used to believe that movement meant progress. That if I wasn't building, fixing, achieving, or proving—I was wasting time. I filled every moment with noise. Music. Work. People. Thoughts. I was terrified of what might surface if I ever stood still long enough to hear it.

But life, in its divine wisdom, has a way of pulling you into stillness—whether you're ready or not.

For me, it came in waves. After the divorce. After heartbreak. After loss. After burnout so heavy it felt like my bones were tired. I had nothing left to offer the world. Not because I didn't want to—but because I had neglected myself for far too long.

And so, I sat in the quiet.

At first, it was agonizing. The silence exposed every wound I tried to ignore. Every lie I believed about myself. Every unhealed part of my story. But something beautiful happened when I stopped resisting it.

I began to listen.

The Difference Between Loneliness and Solitude

Loneliness felt like a wound I couldn't heal. It whispered that I wasn't chosen, that I wasn't enough, that I was forgotten. But solitude? Solitude was a sacred sanctuary.

Loneliness said, *"You're not loved."*
Solitude said, *"Come back home to yourself."*

In solitude, I learned to be with myself—not out of punishment, but devotion. I found calm in candlelit baths and clarity in early morning walks. I discovered that I wasn't as "together" as I appeared, and that was okay. The girl who once thought she had to carry the weight of the world was finally learning to lay it down.

I Wasn't as Polished as I Thought

When I sat with my truth, I saw the masks I had worn: the strong one, the fixer, the high achiever. The one who kept it all together while falling apart inside.

Stillness stripped all of that away. It held up a mirror to my soul. And in that reflection, I saw a woman who didn't need to do more. She needed to feel more.

To be more present. To be more honest. To be more gentle—with herself.

I realized that busyness had become a coping mechanism. It allowed me to avoid grief, avoid disappointment, avoid *me*.

Stillness asked me to be brave enough to feel everything. To stop distracting and start discerning.

It asked me to listen to the parts of me that whispered, *"I'm tired."*

And finally, I listened.

When the World Went Quiet, God Spoke Loudest

In those silent, solitary moments, I didn't feel alone. I felt held.
Not by people. Not by performance. But by presence.
By God. By the Divine. By the version of myself I had long forgotten.

I built a sacred altar—not just in my home, but in my heart. A place where I could come and be honest, messy, soft. A place where I could pray without performance. Cry without apology. Sit without shame.

There, in the quiet, I learned that rest is resistance.
That softness is strength.
That slowing down doesn't mean giving up—it means grounding yourself.
I realized the Universe wasn't punishing me.
It was preserving me.
Teaching me how to stop surviving and start *being*.

Now, I Move Differently

I no longer rush to fix what's uncomfortable. I sit with it.
I no longer fill every space with noise. I honor the quiet.
I no longer fear being alone. I revere it.
Because in stillness, I didn't just find peace.
I found *me*.

The Found Woman Reflection

Affirmation: *"I no longer fear the quiet. In stillness, I hear my truth. In solitude, I meet my soul."*

Journal Prompt: What does stillness reveal to you? Are there parts of your story, your needs, or your healing that you've been avoiding in the noise?

Action Step: Create a sacred "stillness ritual." Choose one moment each day—five minutes or fifty—where you unplug, breathe, and simply *be*. Light a candle. Sit in nature. Close your eyes. No agenda. Just presence.

Found Woman Devotional: "God, Meet Me in the Stillness"

In the hush between heartbeats, the Divine whispers.
Not in thunder or applause, but in breath and awareness.
You are not forgotten in your stillness.
You are remembered.
You are held.
You are home.

God, I spent so much of my life performing—
for love, for safety, for identity.
But here, in the stillness,
I remember who I was before the world told me who to be.

Let silence continue to be my sanctuary.
Let solitude be the sacred soil where I bloom.
Let me stop searching and start listening.
Not for answers, but for presence.

In the quiet, I meet myself again.
And in meeting me, I find You.
Not distant, but dwelling within me.

Today, I do not fill the space.
I allow the space to fill me.
With breath. With truth. With peace.

Amen.

The Found Woman's Path

"Finding yourself is not a one-time event. It's a daily homecoming."

There is no final chapter to becoming. No finish line to healing. I still rise. I still fall. I still listen for the whispers of the woman I've fought so hard to remember.

But now, I don't fear the unraveling. I don't resist the pause. I don't run from the silence. I've learned that the journey inward is sacred—and even in the messiness, there is magic.

To be a Found Woman is not to arrive at a perfect place. It is to stand in your truth. To feel at home in your skin. To speak softly to your soul and mean it.

You are not behind. You are not broken. You are not too late.

You are becoming. Again and again and again.

And that, my sister, is more than enough.

The Found Woman Continues...

Your story is not over.

Let this book be the mirror you hold up to your own journey—your reminder that within you lives a woman who is worthy, radiant, whole, and waiting to be remembered.

May you choose her. Every single day.

Closing Letter to the Reader

Dear Found Woman,

You made it. Through the pain. Through the pages. Through your own moments of remembering.

This journey wasn't just about me—it was about **us**. Every story I shared, every truth I peeled back, was a mirror for you to find your own reflection. The girl you used to be. The woman you're becoming. The one you're still unfolding into.

If you saw yourself in my heartbreak, I pray you also saw yourself in my healing. If you nodded through my confusion, I pray you now feel clarity blooming in your spirit. If you cried through my letting go, I hope you smiled through my rising.

You are not behind. You are not broken. You are not too late.

You are in process. You are in motion. You are becoming.

I don't know where your path leads next—but I do know this: Your softness is strength. Your voice matters. Your dreams are sacred. You are worthy of the life your heart whispers about when it's quiet.

May you never again shrink for love. May you never again silence your soul to keep the peace. May you walk fully in your power, your femininity, your truth.

And when you feel lost again—as we all do from time to time— remember: **You've already found her once. You'll do it again.**

With love,
Latosha S. Bobo

The Found Woman

About the Author

Latosha Bobo is a woman of strength, softness, and spirit. A mother, entrepreneur, real estate professional, and former caregiver turned corporate analyst—her journey has been anything but linear. Through heartbreak, healing, motherhood, and multiple rebirths, Latosha discovered her truest self—not in perfection, but in process.

She is the founder of **Ray of Sunshine Individual Support Services**, a home care agency, and a licensed Realtor helping families build legacies one home at a time through **Select Latosha Homes**. A proud Missouri native, Latosha's passion lies in empowering women, uplifting her community, and using her story to spark transformation.

When she's not advocating for others, you'll find her nurturing her plants, walking in peace, journaling by candlelight, or exploring her spirituality through ancestral wisdom and divine connection.

This is her first book—but certainly not her last.

Follow her journey, connect, or simply say hello:

lbobo@bhhsselectstl.com

Select Latosha Homes

You've spent your life giving, proving, surviving. Now it's time to remember who you are.

If you've ever felt lost in titles, silence, or someone else's idea of who you should be—this book was written for you.

✨ *The Found Woman* is more than a memoir—it's your mirror, your permission slip, your healing companion.

Come home to yourself.
Start reading *The Found Woman* today and begin your own becoming.

👉 Available now on Amazon —
Click here to order your copy.